Riding the Tide

a tithe of psalms **SIMON WARD**

RIVER

My thanks to Richard Walker, Dave McKee and Richard Higginson for wading through the text and giving invaluable feedback; to Deborah Paul for helping with photographs; to Chrissie Abbott, Bianca Harris, Christine and Shane Nearman for their ongoing encouragement; and to my wife Gill, who patiently and lovingly lives out all this stuff with me.

Simon Ward
July 2013

River Publishing & Media Ltd
Barham Court
Teston
Maidstone
Kent
ME18 5BZ
United Kingdom

info@river-publishing.co.uk

Scripture quotations from NIV except where mentioned.

ISBN 978-1-908393-32-6
Printed in the United Kingdom
Photos – most taken by the author on a Canon IXUS 220 HS

contents

introduction

Does anyone need another dissection of the Psalms? Surely enough has already been written. Quite probably, but these reflections are a personal response to a stimulating day spent on Holy Island at Eastertime 2012, which triggered the realisation that I was entering the last decade of my formal working life, and longed to better integrate my Christian faith and the daily round of activity ... whilst there was still time to do something about it.

After three decades working in the creative industries, trying to balance the organised side of who I am (business administrator) with the creative (singer, occasional writer of stuff and worship leader), it seemed right to reflect this by bringing together a variety of disciplines.

As a result, this look at fifteen of the 150 Psalms (10%, thus "Tithe") includes reflections, poems, photos, and each Psalm set to music in a variety of styles (although the music is not included on these pages).

To my surprise, I achieved my somewhat ambitious target of writing the 15 reflections - they were first shared with the HTB Fashion Group on Facebook - setting them to music and memorising them, in 3 months. It was hugely enjoyable, not a task.

As I've then put it all together, a whole pile of other stuff has tumbled in; "prayers through the day" to each Psalm, poems, in depth thoughts on particular Psalms. I hope these will stimulate thought, prayer and, who knows, even action.

The 15 Psalms are grouped into 3 "cycles", paying "tribute" to the fact that much of the music and reflection was dreamed up on my daily trip into work cycling up the A24 through Balham! The first cycle I've entitled "The Big Picture", as the themes span across all of life – God as Creator. Cycle 2, "Intimate Encounters" explores our relationship with God as "lover of our souls". Cycle 3, "Celebrate", focusses on worship of God as Saviour and Lord.

The title reflects the fact that life, like the Psalms, seems to ebb and flow between great and dreadful, beautiful and ugly. The reflections and prayers seek to speak into this ever changing experience. I do hope that you find them an encouragement as you negotiate life's twisting path.

Simon Ward, Spring 2013

Oh how I love Your law! I meditate on it all day long

This first cycle of Psalms seeks to give a feel for some of the big issues that the Bible presents, from the majesty of Creation, mankind's role in overseeing it, a clearly etched distinction between good and evil, the centrality of God's Word, His protection in times of trouble, the apparently upside down values of His Kingdom, and a recognition of the spiritual battle that rages around us. And the Psalms do this in a distinctly personal way that entwines these issues with our everyday lives.

cycle 1
the BIG picture

psalm 1

Blessed is the man who does not walk in the counsel of the wicked or stand in the way of sinners or sit in the seat of mockers. But his delight is in the law of the Lord, and on his law he meditates day and night. He is like a tree planted by streams of water, which yields its fruit in season and whose leaf does not wither - whatever he does prospers.

Not so the wicked! They are like chaff that the wind blows away. Therefore, the wicked will not stand in the judgment, nor sinners in the assembly of the righteous.

For the Lord watches over the way of the righteous, but the way of the wicked will perish.

Holy Island in North East England is an inspiring place, not least for its history. Did you know that, back in the old days, the monks there used to recite the Psalms to each other (they memorised all 150 of them) as they walked from place to place ministering? This sent me back to the Psalms to have a fresh look at how practically relevant they are to our lives today. And I've not been disappointed. Psalm 1 goes straight to the heart of the matter – the importance of immersing ourselves in the Word if we are to walk in God's way for our life. A crystal clear distinction is drawn between the righteous and the wicked. Between those whose lives are like trees firmly rooted by streams of water that bear fruit and don't wither when times get hard ... and dry chaff that is swept away as soon as a wind blows up. No prizes for guessing which is which!

And it is never too late to do something about it. You can't be so dry that, by the transforming power of the Holy Spirit, you cannot be changed (somewhat against the laws of nature!) from chaff to tree. Conversely, trees die off and can become as useless as chaff if they fail to draw sustenance from the River. It's our choice where we let our roots grow.

And this brings me back to those monks, who daily immersed themselves in scripture as they encouraged each other and equipped themselves to be God's hands and feet. They are a wonderful model, regardless of the centuries that separate us, so let's be those who encourage each other to drink deeply of God's Word, and witness how it changes our daily walk and empowers our engagement with God's world.

walk according to the law of the Lord and you will bear fruit and stay strong for the Lord will watch over you

🎼 Your truth never goes out of fashion

Blessed are they whose ways are blameless
who walk according to the law of the Lord
Blessed are they who keep His statutes
And seek Him with all their hearts.

Your truth never goes out of fashion
It stays, as permanent as the heavens.
Your truth never goes out of fashion
I can always walk with my head up high.

My soul faints with longing for your salvation
But I have put my hope in your word
My eyes fail, looking for our promise
I say "When will you comfort me?"

Keep me from deceitful ways
Be gracious to me through Your law
I have chosen the way of truth
I have set my heart on Your laws
I hold fast to Your statutes, O Lord
Do not let me be put to shame
I run in the path of Your commands
For You have set my heart free.

Psalm 119:1-2; 29-32; 81-82 [NIV];
89, 90 [MSG]

A.M. Father God ... good morning. Thank you for looking after me through the watches of the night. Please strengthen my body, calm my feelings, clear my mind and bring alive my spirit as I start a new day. As I read your word draw me to what you have to say to me and grant me boldness to live for You, and You only, as I go out to face the challenges and opportunities the day holds in store.

Father in heaven, hallowed be Your name. Your kingdom come, Your will be done on earth as in heaven. Give me today my daily bread. Forgive me my sins as I forgive those who sin against me, and lead me not into temptation but deliver me from evil. For the Kingdom, the power and the glory are Yours, now and forever, Amen

EVE. Holy Spirit, as the day draws to a close, remind me afresh of the words I read this morning. Open my eyes to what You have been doing through me. Remind me of the Father's promises and how they have held true. Thrill me once more with the majesty of my Lord Jesus.

I pray for those I have come across today who do not know Your love and power. Meet with them and transform their lives. Fill me once more with Your powerful presence so that, daily, I might become more like Jesus. For that is my desire.

Father, Son, Holy Spirit, refresh and restore me. Watch over me and all those who are dear to me this night. Amen.

P.M. Lord Jesus, I'm feeling inadequate today, struggling to hold onto the truth of your word. All those around me don't seem to have the worries I do. When things don't go well, they are quite happy to blame everyone else. I am tempted to join in, but am desperately trying not to. It drains my flagging energy and gets me down.

Yet Lord, I trust that You will indeed bear fruit from my labours. Please sustain me through the remainder of the day and bring alive the promise of your word to prosper whatever I do. Open my eyes to see Your hand at work and bring me home rejoicing at your faithfulness. For your name's sake. Amen.

dogma or conversation?

I love the Bible and I believe it's the key to living life as God planned it. But we do need to consider carefully how we use it in our approach to those unfamiliar with it and who don't yet have a Christian faith. Let me explain.

Psalm 1 is terrific - a real inspiration to countless Christians down the centuries. "Blessed are those ... they will be like trees planted by streams of water ..." The statue in the Courtyard at Somerset House, where I work, has these verses on its base.

But if you are amongst the wicked - ! - Psalm 1 doesn't pan out quite so well and would be a threat and even an affront to you.

So, do we parrot out stuff that's well meant but, with all its talk of the wicked perishing (presumably in a lake of fire), is likely to alienate a new generation from God's amazing grace? Or do we pause to reconsider? It could be a life or death decision – for someone else.

God sent His Son not to condemn but to save. So how do I respond to those who would turn a special day of rest into just another round of frantic activity? What should we say to those who would redefine the God given institution of marriage? Can we agree with anti-Semitists who state that the Jews had their chance, but blew it?

Do I accept an approach that has been handed down from the previous generation? Is sound doctrine enough? Or do I need to re-imagine myself into the footprints of my Creator as He progresses through time with His Creation? Am I prepared to be shown a different way?

But what will we tell? Thou shall not do this or that? Jesus called us to love with all our heart, soul, mind, strength. We must pass on not just words, but deeds. Lives sold out for God, not just in church, but in our homes, neighbourhoods and workplaces.

Today's generation looks for faith in action, conversation, not dogma. Blurting out time honoured "truths" will only alienate.

So, we must handle Psalm 1 with care. Used lovingly, it is a thing of beauty. Handle it insensitively and it becomes a beast.

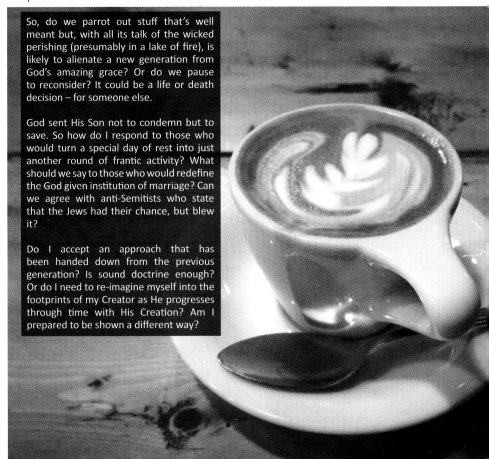

trees

I love trees. Majestic, beautiful, ever changing with the seasons and their maturity. They appear throughout the Bible, symbolising and illustrating God's engagement with His creation.

then all the trees of the forest will sing for joy, they will sing before the Lord. Psalm 96:12

the righteous will flourish like a palm tree. Psalm 92:12

in the middle of the garden were the tree of life and the tree of the knowledge of good and evil. Genesis 2:9b

He is like a tree planted by streams of water which yields its fruit in season and whose leaf does not wither. Whatever he does prospers. Psalm 1:3

The God of our fathers raised Jesus from the dead - whom you had killed by hanging Him on a tree. Acts 5:30

On each side of the river stood the tree of life, bearing twelve crops of fruit, yielding its fruit every month. And the leaves of the tree are for the healing of the nations. Revelation 22:2

psalm 8

what is man that you are mindful of him?

Apparent opposites appear again as they did in Psalm 1. But now we've moved from contrasting the righteous and the wicked to ponder how a majestic God, whose glory lies above the heavens, can notice little old us here on Earth. He does! And what's more, He's given us major responsibility for His Creation. And what's more still, it is the praise of the apparently least influential (mere children) that cuts it in the spiritual realm, silencing those who would set themselves up against God (the wicked, sinners and mockers of Psalm1). And that encourages me, as the world is not short of movers and shakers who set themselves up as the powerful and influential. But those who are truly crowned with glory and honour, and who make a real and lasting difference, are the humble and meek (those infants again) who wonder that God sees them as worthy in the first place. Many I come across day to day lack confidence in their calling and equipping (and that includes me). Chew over Psalm 8, particularly verse 2 ... and allow God to speak to and encourage you - because you're worth it.

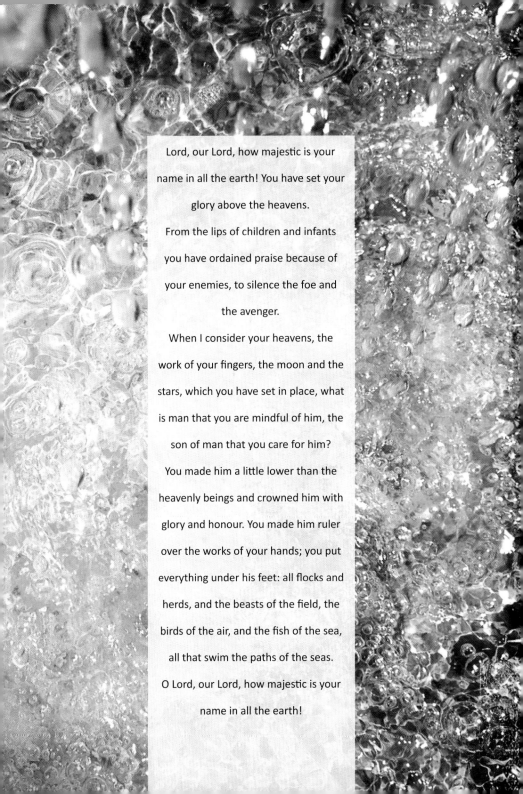

Lord, our Lord, how majestic is your name in all the earth! You have set your glory above the heavens.

From the lips of children and infants you have ordained praise because of your enemies, to silence the foe and the avenger.

When I consider your heavens, the work of your fingers, the moon and the stars, which you have set in place, what is man that you are mindful of him, the son of man that you care for him?

You made him a little lower than the heavenly beings and crowned him with glory and honour. You made him ruler over the works of your hands; you put everything under his feet: all flocks and herds, and the beasts of the field, the birds of the air, and the fish of the sea, all that swim the paths of the seas.

O Lord, our Lord, how majestic is your name in all the earth!

A.M. Father God, as I re-join Your world after a night of rest, I realise afresh that You are so far beyond my comprehension that I am humbled. Your creation, which itself only reflects part of You, is awesome. How small, how insignificant, how helpless am I? And yet you care, indeed love me. That is equally awesome, and humbling. Enable me, this day, to live hour by hour, minute by minute, in the knowledge that I am loved by the Creator Himself. Amen

You have set Your glory above the heavens

P.M. O Lord, I am being blown away today at Your Kingdom rule. I've not spotted any members of the Royal Family walking my streets, but I've seen the King at work in the situations I've been praying for, as if You yourself had been present in person to take charge. Give me, in all my uncertainty, the confidence to know that, though the task ahead can look daunting, the power behind me is bigger still. Rather than seeing myself as a little duck having to paddle hard, help me to understand that, if I trust You to provide, I can be like a ship under full sail carried forward by the wind. O Lord, our Lord, how majestic is your name in all the earth!

EVE. As I look back on my day, I'm glad that I am part of Your family. It's so good to know that You have chosen the likes of me to be Your hands and feet to reach out to a needy world. I admit, it's a bit scary to think that what I do makes a difference, and distinctly worrying that, when I don't do things I know I should, it leaves a gap in Your plan. Sorry, where I've blown it! As I go the bed, please strengthen me so I am ready to please you in all I do tomorrow. Goodnight, Lord.

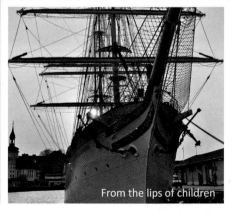

From the lips of children

You crowned
him with glory
and honour

Psalms 8 and 19 both commence with worshipful outbursts in praise of Creation. And Creation is awesomely worthy of our praise. But look closer for, in both Psalms, the writer is quite clear that it is the Creator who is to be worshipped, not that which is created. Creation is a vehicle for the Creator to express Himself and as we explore its awesomeness, variety and pure genius, if you are like me, you will find yourself so astonished at the Being who undertook it, you will shake your head in wonder. This is true and healthy worship.

Worshipping created things is as old as time itself, and we must be wary of looking over our shoulders clucking at how men and women of old could have leapt around poles of wood in a frenzy. But just look at football matches, cars or clothes today. We're still at it! It's the enemy's favourite tactic to imitate, as he is unable to create anything himself. So he entices humankind to focus the worship due to the Creator onto created things which in themselves are quite neutral, and often worthy of admiration, but absolutely not worship.

O Lord, our Lord, how majestic is your name in all the earth!
You have set your glory above the heavens. **Psalm 8:1**

Understanding the distinction between thanksgiving, praise and worship can be helpful. The three terms are often used interchangeably in Christian circles, but they are quite distinct.

Thanksgiving is what it says on the tin; saying thank you for something. We just need to keep our eyes open to see what we should be thankful for and express our gratitude, whether to our fellow citizens or to God. Recognising the cost to the giver, will increase the depth of our thanks.

Praise implies appreciation of giftedness, skill achieved or something well delivered. The more we explore the level of genius or achievement, the greater will be our praise. Again we can rightly praise people, geniuses or not, or God ... and should probably do so more often and generously.

Worship is the highest offering we can give and goes beyond thanks and praise. It involves submission to something or someone higher than ourselves.

The word is often broken into "worth-ship" to help understand the concept behind it - assessing something or someone's worthiness. But something can be worthy of thanks and praise, but not being submitted to. And that's where pictures of Old Testament types on Mount Carmel whirling around wildly to gods of wood and stone appear so ridiculous until we stop and compare them with our modern attitudes to the many material, man-made "gods" that surround us.

No, as Christians we need to recognise that there is only One that qualifies for total submission and therefore true worship; God the Father, God the Son and God the Holy Spirit. Worship Him now.

psalm 19

The heavens declare the glory of God; the skies proclaim the work of his hands. Day after day they pour forth speech; night after night they display knowledge. There is no speech or language where their voice is not heard. Their voice goes out into all the earth, their words to the ends of the world.

In the heavens God has pitched a tent for the sun. It is like a bridegroom coming forth from his pavilion, like a champion rejoicing to run his course. It rises at one end of the heavens and makes its circuit to the other; nothing is hidden from its heat.

The law of the Lord is perfect, reviving the soul. The statutes of the Lord are trustworthy, making wise the simple. The precepts of the Lord are right, giving joy to the heart. The commands of the Lord are radiant, giving light to the eyes. The fear of the Lord is pure, enduring forever. The ordinances of the Lord are sure, and altogether righteous. They are more precious than gold than, much pure gold; they are sweeter than honey than, honey from the comb. By them your servant is warned; in keeping them there is great reward.

But who can discern his errors? Forgive my hidden faults. Keep your servant also from wilful sins; may they not rule over me. Then I will be blameless, innocent of great transgression.

May the words of my mouth and the meditation of my heart be pleasing in your sight, Lord, my Rock and my Redeemer.

The heavens declare the glory of God

Psalm 19 sees an intertwining of Psalms 1 and 8. We are treated to an outburst of praise to God's Creation (Haydn's been here of course for his Creation!). If you're ever stressed (!), take a moment to look up at the skies and the heavens and revel in the awesome, perspective correcting canvas of their Creator.

Then follows a sobering, but Oh So Beautiful plea to dig deep and let the Word transform us into the Person we were made to be. If verses 7-9 appear a tad repetitious, spend more time with them for, as verse 10 reveals, they are more precious than gold and as sweet as honey. Only when we're thus infused (and enthused) by God's Word, will we find true freedom and live in a place of God's pleasure.

Scanning through the expansive sweep of this Psalm, I find myself contemplating what constitutes true beauty - an issue that I and many others who work in fashion frequently ponder. Surely, Godly beauty will be reflected in those who rejoice in the beauty of God's Creation ... and will flow from those whose hearts and lives are shaped by God's Word. Think of someone who is refreshed, wise, joyful, radiant, pure and righteous, not resistant to gentle correction. I'd love to see more and more people looking this sort of gorgeous. Wouldn't you?

through the day with psalm 19

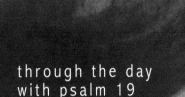

A.M. Father God, my day starts with Your word. As I read, revive me, grant me wisdom, give joy to my heart and light to my eyes; that I might see this day and all that it holds through Your eyes, and live it to the full, to Your glory.

Through the day, Lord, may all the words of my mouth and the meditations of my heart be pleasing in Your sight.

For You are the Rock on which my life is built, and the Redeemer who has bought me at great cost to be part of Your eternal family. Thank you. Amen.

P.M. As I go through my day, Lord Jesus, I see many situations that are not what they seem at first sight; hope, where all seems broken and lost; ugliness that pretends to be beauty. It's so easy to be taken in by initial impressions, but they are so often wrong. Forgive me Lord, where I am drawn in by surface appearances. Help me to search deeper with the insight of the Holy Spirit and the guidance of Your word. Please open my eyes to see true beauty - beauty of character, selflessness of action, nobility of character. Protect me from "going with the crowd " and pandering to falsehood.

EVE. As the day draws to a close, I want to thank you, Father God, for your marvellous world; the beauty of creation in its rich variety and glorious majesty; almost unseen examples of people doing beautiful things without seeking reward; the truthfulness of Your word which remains true and endures forever.

Against all this, search me Lord for hidden faults and forgive me for things I have done that are blatantly wrong. Cleanse me that I might become an ever more true reflection of my wonderful Saviour, King and Friend, Jesus Christ. And I can only ask it in His name. Amen.

Start the Day with God

Psalm 19 gives a perfect framework for some early morning time with God. Check it out and let it be your guide. Try this suggestion.

Once you've brushed your teeth and made yourself respectable, don't allow your head to drop at the prospect of the day ahead. Look out of the window and up at the sky. It may be glorious sunshine or chucking it down.

Whatever's going on, ponder which aspect of God's character is being played out before you, for "the heavens declare the glory of God, the skies proclaim the work of His hands." (1-4a) Enjoy what comes to mind and worship this matchless Creator.

At this point, I often find myself drifting into the day and what it holds in store (usually accompanied by some worrying). Grasp hold of verses 4b-6, which track the sun's progress "like a champion rejoicing to run his course". Are you feeling threatened by what lies ahead or are you "like a bridegroom coming forth from his pavilion", alive with anticipation?

Try aligning your outlook with the joyful curve of the day's rhythm as the sun makes its way through the sky. When we fix our eyes on our Creator, there will be a sense of direction, purpose and security about where our day is leading, regardless of whether sun, storm or shower prevails.

And then it's time for God's Word (7-10). This daily bread is more important than breakfast and what you discover as you read and wait will be "sweeter than honey". Allow it to explore every aspect of who you are and what you do.

This will be a challenge as your eyes are lifted from the focus on self which leads to the error, faults and sin of verses 11-13. Go with it, be warned and accept forgiveness.

This done, you'll find that the words of your mouth and the meditation of your heart (and what you do and how) pleasing to God (14).

At which point, you're ready to face the day and all it has in store, including breakfast. Nice one.

The heavens declare the glory of God

The skies proclaim the work of His hands

Day after day they pour forth speech

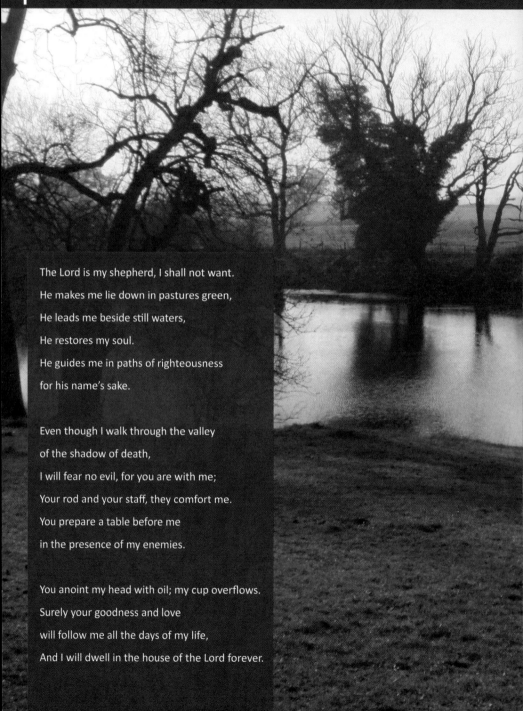

psalm 23

The Lord is my shepherd, I shall not want.

He makes me lie down in pastures green,

He leads me beside still waters,

He restores my soul.

He guides me in paths of righteousness

for his name's sake.

Even though I walk through the valley

of the shadow of death,

I will fear no evil, for you are with me;

Your rod and your staff, they comfort me.

You prepare a table before me

in the presence of my enemies.

You anoint my head with oil; my cup overflows.

Surely your goodness and love

will follow me all the days of my life,

And I will dwell in the house of the Lord forever.

Psalm 23 wraps welcome encouragement and reassurance around a centre of unwanted, darker days of testing that we all will have to cope with at some stage and, indeed, stand with those who are in the thick of it. These times will see us having to respond to the evil around us, confront our enemies and traverse "the valley of the shadow of death" - in which I guess can lurk day to day physical, mental and spiritual struggles through to life threatening illness, death itself and coping with bereavement. Difficult places to be.

The key to making it through, the Psalm tells us, is to believe that our Lord is indeed with us as He says He will be; going before us, walking alongside and, on occasion, simply picking us up and carrying us like any shepherd would his sheep. And of course, Jesus has been through the worst that life can throw at anyone and emerged victorious, so throwing our lot in with Him is anything but blind optimism.

Quite the opposite, it is a considered response to One who will supply all our needs; a choice that we will find all the more natural if we have spent those times of restoration with the Good Shepherd as He leads us by still waters and along paths of righteousness. (A quick workplace moment here, as it can be a driven and stressful place and we risk missing out on these times of refreshment unless we seek them, Him, quite intentionally.)

The outcome, in this life and through eternity, is as secure as it is mind blowing - "His goodness and love will follow me all the days of my life, and I will dwell in the house of the Lord for ever". I've been setting the Psalms to music as I've been considering them, and these last verses, in spite of their darker predecessors, led me to end with an outburst of joyful praise - for that's the way it will be! Hallelujah, what a Saviour!

He leads me beside still waters, He restores my soul

Lunchtime Office

I've been thrilled, courtesy of the Northumbria Community, to discover the historic devotional activity known as the Daily Office. With an intentional play on words, I have tried to adapt it to my working day by leaving the office each lunch break to spend time on my Daily Office. The aim, simply, is to create space with God in the morning, mid-day and evening, for a purposeful break from normal activity to re-focus on, listen to and talk with God. It takes me 15 minutes or so to still my body, quieten my mind and open my spirit to God and what He wishes to share with me. I sometimes drop into St Clement Danes on the Strand (the RAF church and of oranges and lemons fame), one of six churches within 5 minutes of where I work and where I try to escape to as many days during the week as I can.

Here's one example of how I use the time. First five minutes sitting quietly, looking around and letting my eyes fall on what they will. On this particular day, I noticed the nine books of remembrance where all 125,000 RAF personnel who have lost their lives in active service are listed. Across the church were two women looking at an opened cabinet searching, I presumed, for the name of a loved one who had died. In turn, this reminded me of the statue outside the church of Bomber Harris who, regardless of what you think of the raids on Dresden at the end of WW2 that gained him his nickname, must have shown incredible steadfastness of purpose to send men to likely death. And then there were the thousands of civilians on the ground who were killed.

That's more than enough material for the next 10 or 15 minutes. I reflected on the love of our Father God who sent His only son, Jesus to live amongst us, and the steadfastness He showed as He allowed His Son to die for us. I pondered my own steadfastness of purpose as a Christian in my workplace and prayed for courage to be a worthy witness to my sacrificial Father. I moved on to pray for all servicemen who risk their lives and the families of those who find themselves bereaved, often losing sons, husbands, wives, sisters, brothers, daughters at a young age and often with young children. I reflected on those who are innocent victims of war and tried to imagine what it was like and prayed for those who suffer today.

I moved on to pray for my own afternoon's engagements and by the time I was walking back to the office, I was in a very different place with my Father and my neighbour.

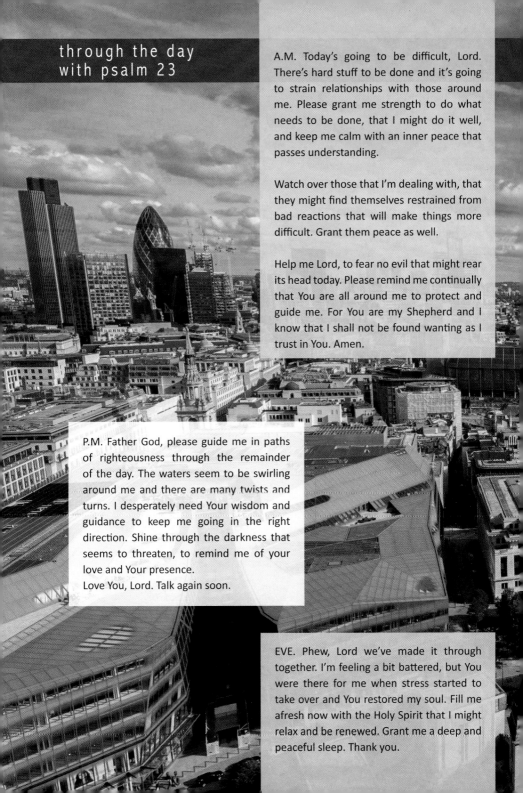

through the day
with psalm 23

A.M. Today's going to be difficult, Lord. There's hard stuff to be done and it's going to strain relationships with those around me. Please grant me strength to do what needs to be done, that I might do it well, and keep me calm with an inner peace that passes understanding.

Watch over those that I'm dealing with, that they might find themselves restrained from bad reactions that will make things more difficult. Grant them peace as well.

Help me Lord, to fear no evil that might rear its head today. Please remind me continually that You are all around me to protect and guide me. For You are my Shepherd and I know that I shall not be found wanting as I trust in You. Amen.

P.M. Father God, please guide me in paths of righteousness through the remainder of the day. The waters seem to be swirling around me and there are many twists and turns. I desperately need Your wisdom and guidance to keep me going in the right direction. Shine through the darkness that seems to threaten, to remind me of your love and Your presence.
Love You, Lord. Talk again soon.

EVE. Phew, Lord we've made it through together. I'm feeling a bit battered, but You were there for me when stress started to take over and You restored my soul. Fill me afresh now with the Holy Spirit that I might relax and be renewed. Grant me a deep and peaceful sleep. Thank you.

psalm 27

The Lord is my light and my salvation - whom shall I fear? The Lord is the stronghold of my life, of whom shall I be afraid? When evil men advance against me to devour me, when my enemies and my foes attack me, they will stumble and fall. Though an army besiege me, my heart will not fear; though war break out against me, even then I will be confident.

One thing I ask from the Lord, this only do I seek: that I may dwell in the house of the Lord all the days of my life, to gaze on the beauty of the Lord and to seek him in his temple. For in the day of trouble he will keep me safe in his dwelling; He will hide me in the shelter of his sacred tent and set me high upon a rock. Then my head will be exalted above the enemies who surround me; at his sacred tent I will sacrifice with shouts of joy I will sing and make music to the Lord.

Hear my voice when I call, Lord; be merciful to me and answer me. My heart says of you, "Seek his face!" Your face, Lord, I will seek.

Do not hide your face from me, do not turn your servant away in anger; you have been my helper. Do not reject me or forsake me, God my Saviour. Though my father and mother forsake me, the Lord will receive me.

Teach me your way, O Lord; lead me in a straight path because of my oppressors. Do not hand me over to the desire of my foes, for false witnesses rise up against me, breathing malicious accusations.

I am still confident of this: I will see the goodness of the Lord in the land of the living. Wait for the Lord; be strong and take heart and wait for the Lord.

Though an army besiege me,
my heart will not fear

It takes a while to see what's going on in Psalm 27. Having to persevere turns out to be integral to its message, though, as the repeated exhortation of the last verse - "Wait for the Lord" - spells out. I have sometimes found myself being challenged as appearing indecisive in the workplace when stating that I want to "get my head round" an issue before taking a decision. I disagree. There is great benefit in pausing to wait, in my case on the Lord, when too often it can be easy to race ahead or allow ourselves to be pushed into something before we're ready. (Check out a great book by Stephen Cottrell – "Hit the ground kneeling") This may not always be popular to a worldly (driven) mindset, but many a wrong decision is taken in haste and relationships are so easily damaged by a quick comeback (beware emails).

The Psalm encourages us that, as we wait for the Lord, we will see His goodness, but we need to be strong and take heart as we will be going against the tide. There again, in our "I want it now" culture, we can seek instant gratification by laying our hands quickly on lots of stuff but, in settling for this, we may never hang around long enough to experience deeper things.

How does all this play out in Psalm 27? The psalmist is under attack, serious attack, but the first thing he does is not to go on the offensive, but to reflect quietly on the blessings of dwelling in the house of the Lord and, gazing on His beauty, ie worship, he seeks God's face. What emerges is that, whilst worshipping, the psalmist finds not only blessing, but also security ... and victory. All this is subversively counter-cultural, even counter-intuitive, but it is the way of a Lord who slept in a boat while all around panicked at the engulfing storm.

Bless the Lord, O my soul, and worship His holy name.

through the day with psalm 27

One thing I ask ...

A.M. Father God, please open my eyes today to see Your beauty in the world around me - however unobvious it might be at first sight. Keep me from rushing around so much that I'm oblivious to everything and everyone around me.

Help me to weigh carefully each decision, inviting Your perspective at all times. Protect me from being steamrollered into things.

Teach me Your way, O Lord, in all I do, so that I might see Your goodness at work throughout the day. Amen.

... to gaze on the beauty of the Lord

P.M. I'm feeling under pressure today, Lord, and it's always difficult to know whether there's a hand behind it all, or it's just the way things have gone.

Regardless, I call out to You, and ask that you will keep me safe, that You will "set me high upon a rock", out of the reach of those who would do me harm. I'm imagining myself safe in the house of the Lord, where I am seeking Your face in the midst of the day's busyness.

I remain confident that You are my stronghold, my light and my salvation. Thank you.

... to seek Him in His temple

EVE. Yes Lord, You have come through again. You have not hidden Your face from me. It's only when I forget to look up to You, that things tend to go pear shaped. Sorry for when that's happened.

As I look back on the day, I rejoice that You continue to lift me up.

... with shouts of joy, I will sing and make music to the Lord.

With the Psalmist, I want to offer you a sacrifice of thanks with a shout of joy and music in my heart. You are the stronghold of my life, of whom shall I be afraid? No one!

I will wait quietly now to hear Your words of comfort and strength as I prepare for bed. Thank you.

Psalm 27 is a blockbuster, opening the window onto a world of spiritual awareness, discernment and warfare.

Whilst this is not territory encountered by many of us, it is nonetheless there, around us all the time, with activity ranging from "casual" psychic dalliances with Tarot cards and Ouija boards to powerful and life changing movings of the Holy Spirit.

It is a place where, as in the classic CS Lewis tale, The Lion the Witch and the Wardrobe, there are two quite distinct kingdoms: eternal truth and passing counterfeit.

Scary stuff! And it's tempting not to want to enter this world (as the children in the tale unwittingly did through the wardrobe). Indeed, looking back at Psalm 27, there's nothing vaguely "sensible" about a Psalm that urges us not to be fearful of an armed siege, let alone being confident as war breaks out against us. Do we really want to go there?

But if we steer clear, free rein (and reign) will be given to those who knowingly exercise spiritual power outside the direction of the Holy Spirit. And then others, being assured that it's only a bit of fun, will be at greater risk of finding themselves drawn into something far darker and more dangerous than they ever imagined.

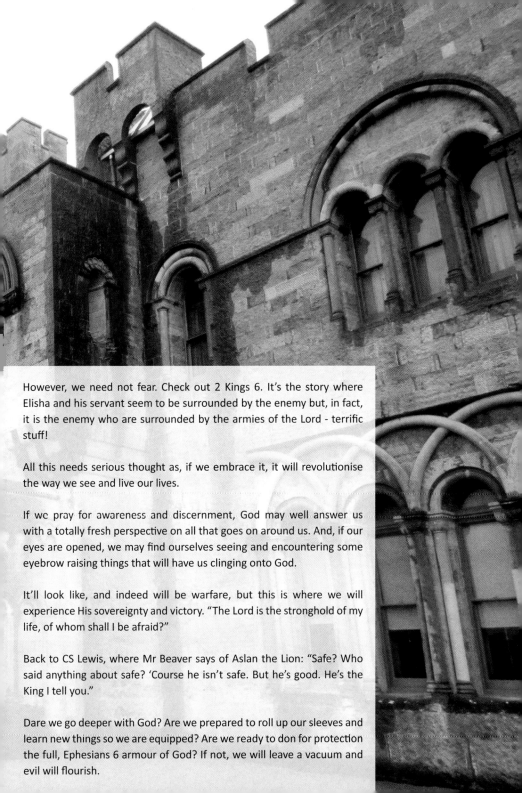

However, we need not fear. Check out 2 Kings 6. It's the story where Elisha and his servant seem to be surrounded by the enemy but, in fact, it is the enemy who are surrounded by the armies of the Lord - terrific stuff!

All this needs serious thought as, if we embrace it, it will revolutionise the way we see and live our lives.

If we pray for awareness and discernment, God may well answer us with a totally fresh perspective on all that goes on around us. And, if our eyes are opened, we may find ourselves seeing and encountering some eyebrow raising things that will have us clinging onto God.

It'll look like, and indeed will be warfare, but this is where we will experience His sovereignty and victory. "The Lord is the stronghold of my life, of whom shall I be afraid?"

Back to CS Lewis, where Mr Beaver says of Aslan the Lion: "Safe? Who said anything about safe? 'Course he isn't safe. But he's good. He's the King I tell you."

Dare we go deeper with God? Are we prepared to roll up our sleeves and learn new things so we are equipped? Are we ready to don for protection the full, Ephesians 6 armour of God? If not, we will leave a vacuum and evil will flourish.

The second cycle gets personal
and explores the light and shade
of the Psalms as the writers
pour out their souls to God
... often with considerable
forthrightness.

cycle 2

close
encounters

psalm 42

As the deer pants for streams of water,

so my soul pants for you, my God.

My soul thirsts for God, for the living God.

When can I go and meet with God?

My tears have been my food day and night,

while men say to me all day long,

"Where is your God?"

These things I remember as I pour out my soul:

how I used to go to with the multitude

Leading the procession to the house of God

with shouts of joy and thanksgiving

among the festive throng.

Why are you downcast, O my soul?

Why so disturbed within me?

Put your hope in God, for I will yet praise him,

my Saviour and my God. My soul is downcast

within me; therefore I will remember you

from the land of the Jordan,

 the heights of Hermon - from Mount Mizar.

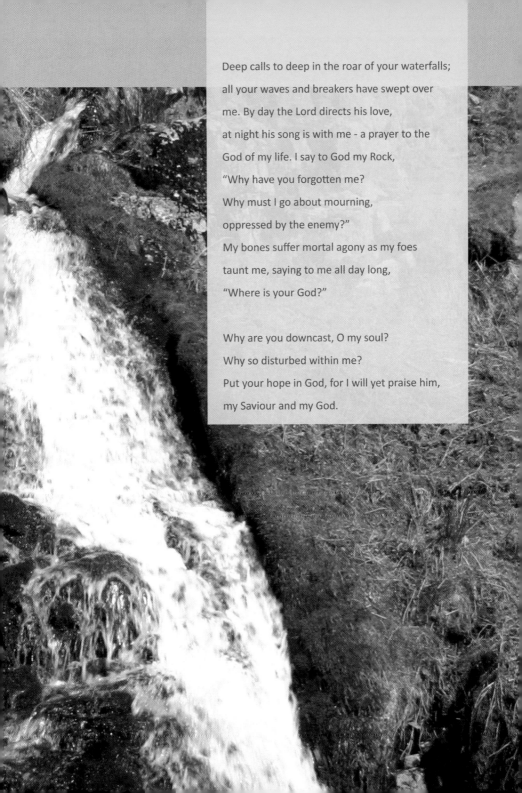

Deep calls to deep in the roar of your waterfalls;
all your waves and breakers have swept over
me. By day the Lord directs his love,
at night his song is with me - a prayer to the
God of my life. I say to God my Rock,
"Why have you forgotten me?
Why must I go about mourning,
oppressed by the enemy?"
My bones suffer mortal agony as my foes
taunt me, saying to me all day long,
"Where is your God?"

Why are you downcast, O my soul?
Why so disturbed within me?
Put your hope in God, for I will yet praise him,
my Saviour and my God.

Journey to the The Waterfall

Destination selected,
Route planned,
Day decided,
Weather forecast ignored.
Breakfast, layer up, set off.
Wrong turns taken,
Car park found – eventually.
Shoes off, boots on,
Quick loo visit,
We're ready to go.

Half hour's walk along muddy path,
Wet drizzle becomes wetter rain -
This is Wales, so no complaints!
Meander alongside bubbling waters,
Clambering, slipping over lifted roots.
Climbing steeply, leaving stream behind.
Enter dripping woodland,
Skies grow darker.
Check map, retrace steps,
Is this the right path now?
Still through dripping woodland.

Onward trek as rain get serious.
Then, at first felt more than heard,
A gentle shaking –
Thunder? Even heavier rain?
Well wrapped up, so we'll survive.
Gentle roar is steadily growing.
Ah! Is this the waterfall?
Surprising that it rumbles so.

Zig zag downwards,
Slipping, sliding.
Then, approaching precipitous bend,
Through leafless branches,
Partly seen, part imagined,
There she is. Majestic.

What is it about waterfalls?
Mesmerising movement,
Something wild, untamed,
Yet dangerously beautiful.
Silently slipping
Over smooth precipice,
Breaking, cascading,
A downward torrent.
Crashing, roaring
Into the river below
Clouds of spray.
Strangely mysterious.

So, now I'm here,
What am I expecting?
Has it been worth the hike?
The mud, the wet, the puff?
Why have I come?
To measure drop or width?
To gauge water flow?
To enjoy peace and quiet?
Certainly isn't quiet.
And it's very wet!

Close eyes, breathe deep.
Quiet, still, pause.
Now look again.

One small corner
Of amazing creation.

And I am changed.
Stresses, worries fall away.
Sort of not relevant here.

In their stead come space,
Fullness, hope, joy.
Release.

Thank you, Waterfall.
Good to spend time with you.

"Downcast Praise" may sound a bit odd and potentially an oxymoron, but the briefest of scans through the Psalms quickly reveals just as much heartbreak and complaint as exuberance and joy. But it's all in praise of a God who's not fazed by anything we throw at Him. Now, to me at least, this comes as a big relief - we don't have to set a fixed grin before we can praise God.

Tears, and indeed anguished protest, are welcomed equally by God. Verses 7-10 are well known, and their mysteriousness somehow blends together great beauty and loud protest; "Deep calls to deep ... Your waves and breakers have swept over me ... why have you forgotten me, why must I go about mourning, oppressed by the enemy, my bones suffer mortal agony as my foes taunt me ...".

This is not cheerful stuff, but it is engagement with God, worship, at the deepest and most heartfelt level.

And I believe this should be a huge inspiration, particularly if you are a creative and likely to plumb the depths more deeply and often than those with a more prosaic outlook on life. Beauty (and let's not confuse it with pretty - rugged and terrifying rock faces can be beautiful) can be quite at home in a place of raw pain and confusion and we need to grant ourselves permission, as David and the other psalmists did, to let rip on God.

This will not just act as a safety valve when we're on the fraught side, but will open a door to knowing our real selves and discovering just how close God (and Jesus who, of course, has been there and got the t-shirt) stands alongside us through all the joys and sorrows of life's journey.

The key to making sense of all this is not to bash ourselves about with positive thinking (which has its limitations at the best of times), but is set out in the refrain "Why are you downcast, O my soul? Why so disturbed within me? Put your hope in God, for I will yet praise Him, my Saviour and my God." Our strength for times of trouble is built up in a quieter place where we can grow our relationship with God and let this blossom into trust, which in turn leads to hope when the heat's on.

Downcast
Praise

A.M. Father God, I've been feeling really downhearted recently and You seem to be distant. Please remind me afresh of your goodness; the blessings you have poured out on me; the fact that I am your adopted son, part of a royal priesthood. Inspire me again with Your purpose for my life.

I long to feel Your love - not just to know it in my mind. Even though I am downcast, and I am feeling nothing but a grey dullness, I will put my hope in You, Lord. I'm going to trust that, stepping out in the truth of Your love and goodness, You will set me free afresh, to praise You with joy and gladness – for You are my Saviour and my God. Turn my mourning into dancing and my greyness into vibrant colour.

P.M. Lord Jesus, I am trying to hold onto You today, but it's not easy. I'm sensing that those around me are making my life difficult and I'm not liking it. Pour out on me Your grace, that I might be gracious to others and gentle on myself.

Remind me of times not long past when the sun seemed to be shining brightly on me. I know it's still there, but it seems to be behind dark clouds. Break out Lord and let the sunshine of Your love beam down on me once again.

Refresh me Lord for the remainder of the day, strengthen me to keep going and grant me a peace that passes understanding. Amen

EVE. At night, His song is with me - a prayer to the God of my life ...

I have heard a thousand songs, listened to a thousand tongues, but there is one that sounds above them all. The Father's song, The Father's love, You sung it over me and for eternity, it's written on my heart. Heaven's perfect melody, the Creator's symphony, You are singing over me, The Father's song. Heaven's perfect mystery, the King of Love has sent for me, and now You're singing over me, the Father's song.

The Father's Song
by Matt Redman

Father God, it's mystery all, but I place my trust in You, this night and forever. Good night.

Oh Dear Day

Today's an "Oh dear" day, Lord. I have a busy diary, full of challenges, but I'm feeling weary and down, and I really don't feel up to it at all. And all my well-honed doubts and insecurities come swarming over me like unwelcome relations arriving for Christmas. Am I up to all this? Am I in the right place? Should I get out?

I know I have to ignore these voices, which drag me down. When push comes to shove, I must simply get on with what's before me, regardless of how I'm feeling. And I know I should be so past letting this predictable stuff get to me. But it still does, and it's such an upsetting place to be, so draining. I'm wanting to be an effective ambassador for my business, a good role model for those who look to me, a faithful and joyful witness to an all powerful God of love who equips His people for the task ahead. Oh dear!

But enough of inward looking melancholy. I look to You, Lord: Who gives strength to do all things; Who equips those He calls; Who is faithful and true.

I will be still before You and know that You are God. Encourager, Empathiser, Healer, Provider, Advocate, Intercessor, Victor, Game Changer ... seated right now at the right hand of the Father. Yet nothing is too trivial for You, and certainly not too tricky. You've been here. You've got the T-shirt.

I name all this stuff for what it is: a lie. And I place myself and my day before You, Lord. I trust all that I have to do, all the people I will meet, and myself, into Your hands. With confidence.

Amen and Hallelujah.

Put your hope in God,
for I will yet praise Him

God is our refuge and strength, an ever-present help in trouble. Therefore we will not fear, though the earth give way and the mountains fall in to the heart of the sea,
though its waters roar and foam and the mountains quake with their surging.

There is a river whose streams make glad the city of God, the holy place where the Most High dwells. God is within her, she will not fall; God will help her at break of day. Nations are in uproar, kingdoms fall; he lifts his voice, the earth melts. The Lord Almighty is with us; the God of Jacob is our fortress.

Come and see what the Lord has done, the desolations he has brought on the earth. He makes wars cease to the ends of the earth. He breaks the bow and shatters the spear; he burns the shields with fire.

He says "Be still, and know that I am God; I will be exalted among the nations, I will be exalted in the earth." The Lord Almighty is with us; the God of Jacob is our fortress.

An observation I heard several times in the run up to the Diamond Jubilee weekend in June 2012 was that the Queen represents stability at a time of rapid and often bewildering change. Psalm 46 takes us into similar territory. The best known verse - "Be still, and know that I am God" - sounds as if it belongs in Psalm 23. But it actually follows a cataclysmic catalogue of destruction and uproar in nature and human affairs.

So what on earth is it doing here? Surely, if the world is collapsing around us, terror is entirely warranted. But no, we are urged not to fear. Rather, taking refuge in the same God who is bringing desolation to the earth, we are directed to lift our eyes to the promise of a future in God's very presence.

In doing so, we open ourselves to the realisation that the same God is right here beside us in the middle of life's conflicts - which takes us back to "Be still, and know that I am God". In the turmoil of modern life - was it ever actually any different?! - we won't know the security of living under God's protection until we consciously take charge of ourselves and focus our attention on He who is in charge of all things.

There's no suggestion here of an easy going "let go and let God" philosophy. "Be still" is a command. If we do not take heed, we will fail to grow in our knowledge of God and His ways. And, to boot, we risk being consumed in the battle that rages around us. Just as silence is one of God's most precious gifts, stillness is a doorway through which we enter His presence. Get in there, for God is our refuge and strength!

Be still
and know
that I
am God

A.M. This is one of my favourite "be still" pictures - the beautiful lake at Petworth House created by the master of landscaping, Capability Brown. The lake combines nature and man's efforts, and that's where we will find real stillness; when we place ourselves quite intentionally before God .... to feel his breath and hear His voice.

Father God, at the start of a new day, before I get drawn into a round of distracting activity, I come before You in quietness; to sense Your presence, to feel Your breath of love, to hear Your still, quiet voice speaking into my life.

Speak Lord, I am listening.

P.M. Lord, quieten me once more, I pray, that I may regain poise and focus. I lay before You the things that have knocked me off balance this morning. Sorry I am so easily wrong footed. Here I am again, use this time as You will Lord. I will wait for You.

EVE. Isn't there something special about water and trees? Think back to Psalm 1, where the blessed person is likened to a tree planted by streams of water that yields it fruit in season and whose leaf does not wither.

And then, similar to the imagery of Psalm 46, water and trees can be lashed by wind and rain, but when the storm passes, their stability and strength enables them to return to a place of calm.

Marvel in a favourite stretch of water or tree and ponder the Creator who made them.

Then be still before God.

There is a river, whose streams make glad the city of God

psalm 51

Have mercy on me, O God, according to your unfailing love; according to your great compassion blot out my transgressions. Wash away all my iniquity and cleanse me from my sin. For I know my transgressions, and my sin is always before me.

Against you, you only, have I sinned and done what is evil in your sight; so you are right in your verdict and justified when you judge. Surely I was sinful at birth, sinful from the time my mother conceived me. Yet you desired faithfulness even in the womb; you taught me wisdom in that secret place.

Cleanse me with hyssop, and I will be clean; wash me, and I will be whiter than snow. Let me hear joy and gladness; let the bones you have crushed rejoice. Hide your face from my sins and blot out all my iniquity.

Create in me a pure heart, O God, and renew a steadfast spirit within me. Do not cast me from your presence or take your Holy Spirit from me.

Restore to me the joy of your salvation and grant me a willing spirit, to sustain me. Then I will teach transgressors your ways, so that sinners will turn back to you. Deliver me from the guilt of bloodshed, O God, you who are God my Saviour, and my tongue will sing of your righteousness.

Open my lips, Lord, and my mouth will declare your praise. You do not delight in sacrifice, or I would bring it; you do not take pleasure in burnt offerings. My sacrifice, O God, is a broken spirit; a broken and contrite heart you, God, will not despise.

May it please you to prosper Zion, to build up the walls of Jerusalem. Then you will delight in the sacrifices of the righteous, in burnt offerings offered whole; then bulls will be offered on your altar.

Against You, You only, have I sinned

Psalm 51 is tough to handle. It deals with sin, guilt, forgiveness and restoration, areas none of us find easy. Written by David after his adultery with Bathsheba followed by the murder of her husband, he couldn't have sunk much lower - and this is the great King of Israel, God's chosen people, and the legendary Psalmist.

But it's not that I find myself asking "how on earth could he have got it so wrong" - anyone knowing a little of themselves will recognise how easily we can slip and fall. It's what follows that I have to grapple with.

Let me explain. We sin (not good); we feel guilty (good, at least our conscience is intact); we confess all to a gracious God (wonderful that we can do so); we are forgiven (as a result of the sacrifice of an amazing Saviour, thank you); we move on ... aha, here's the sticking point.

Wash me, and I will be whiter than snow

If you're like me, you don't find it that easy to let go of the regret and downheartedness you feel when you've got it wrong. You dwell on who you've hurt along the way.

Psalm 51 offers a model of how to move on. It reveals a process at work, one that will not be easy or happen overnight, and which goes through several phases which are set out below in "Sin and restoration".

There's no quick fix or short cut here, any more than there was cheap grace to enable forgiveness in the first place. But it's worth it, as un-forgiveness and staying in a place of separation from God and others is one of the most debilitating things to endure. Father God, restore to me the joy of your salvation.

Amen.

A.M. Jesus my Saviour, I want to start the day with a clean heart.

In the quiet of the morning, please bring to mind the things that I have been getting wrong over the last few days. Help me to name them, one by one. I place them at the foot of Your cross and ask for Your forgiveness.

Cleanse me with hyssop and I will be clean, wash me and I will be whiter than snow. Amen.

Have mercy on me, O God according to Your unfailing love, cleanse me from my sin for I know my transgressions.

Open my lips, Lord, and my mouth
will declare Your praise

P.M. Lord, it makes such a difference when I have come before You and unloaded all the mess that can clog up my life. Thank you that You are faithful and just and forgive us our sins.

Where I tend to hang onto my guilt, please set me free to rejoice, as it is by Your grace that I am pardoned and set free, not what I have earned.

Give me courage to share the good things You have done for me. Thank you. Amen.

Restore to me the joy of Your salvation then I will teach transgressors Your ways. Deliver me from the guilt of bloodshed and my tongue will sing of Your righteousness

EVE. I'm not quite over it yet, Lord, but I know that my heart is right with You now, so I'm going to let rip in praise anyway.

Bless the Lord, O my soul, Worship His holy name. Sing like never before, O my soul, And worship His holy name.

Bless the Lord, O my soul
by Matt Redman

My sacrifice, O Lord is a broken spirit;
a broken and contrite heart You, God, will not despise

Psalm 51 is not skimmed milk for easy digestion. It's a solid steak that requires serious chewing. But if we're prepared to get stuck in, the nourishment is proportionately the greater. It has been challenging to get a grip on, but this is hardly surprising when it expresses an outpouring of anguish at the realisation of responsibility for a double catastrophe - adultery compounded by murder. It then sweeps on through original sin, a model restoration process, and concludes with bull sacrifice. Not the everyday stuff of 21st century life. Is it relevant?

Let's start with those bulls. I wish the last couple of verses weren't there, as they ruin the poetic flow of a psalm that carries us from realisation, confession and cleansing through to forgiveness and restoration - a timeless process that can help guide us out of dark valleys and into sunlit plains. But suddenly we're dropped, unceremoniously (!), into the intricacies of Old Testament religious practice and it seems a million miles away. But - and this is part of the excitement of discovery in many of the psalms where the connections at first seem annoyingly obscure - it turns out to be entirely relevant. So please stay with me.

Firstly, let's be clear - orthodox religious practice is good. Whether established in Leviticus or the Articles of the Church of England, it was introduced to help normal people honour God in their everyday lives.

However, like much that outlasts those who first adopt it, the essence can easily be lost and an empty shell left which, without the substance, misses the original point. We must be wise to this, and take care not to throw out the baby with the bath water.

Back to the bulls, burnt offerings were set up on God's direct instruction, through Moses and executed by Aaron, as a sacrifice for the sin of God's people (Leviticus 16). This is good stuff and foreshadowed the substitutionary sacrifice of Jesus on the cross. (Ask the Vicar if you need to understand more about "substitutionary" sacrifice). The idea, of course, was that the sacrifice was an outward sign of an inward action. In other words, the people were sorry that they'd got stuff wrong and the sacrifice was a visible expression of their confession. Without genuine sorrow and confession, however, the sacrifice was meaningless, a hollow gesture.

And this is what the psalmist is drawing attention to in verse 16, "You do not delight in sacrifice, or I would bring it; you do not take pleasure in burnt offerings." God was rejecting their sacrifices, not because He'd changed his mind and bulls were no longer flavour of the month. Rather, He was responding to the fact that the outward act had replaced any meaningful inward reality. And Psalmist David is quite clear in verse 17, "My sacrifice, O God, is a broken spirit; a broken and contrite heart you, God, will not despise." Then in verses 18 and 19, with genuine confession back on the table, the sacrifice of bulls is back on the menu.

Scanning through the Psalm, we can then see how this is a relevant epilogue, a concluding lesson maybe, to what has gone before. David (2 Samuel 11) had committed his double sin and was getting on with life hoping nobody would spot what had happened.

Until, that is, the prophet Nathan turned up and blew the whistle (2 Samuel 12). David had probably apologised to Bathsheba for having to murder her husband and he may even have said a quick sorry to God for getting it all wrong. But it was not a true recognition of what had happened. Nor was it heartfelt confession. It was only when the enormity of what he'd done and, indeed, his innate sinfulness, came to light in the depths of his soul, that he realised his sin was against God and Psalm 51 poured out.

Do we take sin seriously? Do we seriously believe that we are shot through with sinfulness and have been so since before birth? Verses 5 & 6 read poetically, but they make it crystal clear that we are born at odds with God. We've arrived at original sin here - again if you need help, call the Vicar! Original sin is a big issue, but one thing it tells us is that it's not just dodgy actions that need clearing up with God. It's who we are and have always been. The quality of our relationship with God is what counts, not the quantity of our misdeeds. As I learnt in Sunday School, I is at the centre of SIN! If we think it's just what we do that gets between God and us, we're missing the point and we'll forever be getting it wrong.

And then, do we breeze into God's presence totally oblivious to the fact that He is an all seeing and holy God who won't listen to our songs and prayers when we have (hopefully just) proverbial blood on our hands? Do we "sacrifice bulls" by offering worship, taking communion, pretending all is well with family and friends when, in fact, it is not? Do we need a Nathan to confront us with our need of forgiveness? Are we sufficiently in touch with the indwelling Holy Spirit to be attuned to who we are and how we live our daily lives?

Sin is serious and cannot be overlooked by God until it is dealt with. We cannot remain on the throne of our lives and expect our relationship with God to flourish.

Once we've identified our sin and sinfulness, do we stubbornly refuse to repent, and wonder why we know no peace? Psalm 51 sets out a clear process for moving on - from bondage to freedom; darkness to light; separation to restoration; unwillingness to witness; tongue-tied-ness to praise. Here's the process:

1. COME CLEAN WITH GOD.
"Against you and you only have I sinned". He knows, of course, but it's us who need to open our eyes and hearts to what's happened.

2. CARRY OUT A THOROUGH CLEAN UP.
"Cleanse me" (scrub with soap) and "wash me" (rinse off the dirt released by the soap). This entails coming to the foot of the cross and laying our sin there.

3. RECEIVE RESTORATION.
"Create in me a pure heart", "Renew a steadfast spirit", "Restore to me joy", "Grant me a willing spirit". This stage will need serious time spent with God as we ask Him to "deliver me from guilt".

4. PRESS ON TO PRAISE AND WITNESS.
Then, and only then, will we be able to move forward. "My tongue will sing of your righteousness", "Open my lips and my mouth will declare your praise". "Then I will teach transgressors your ways, so that sinners will turn back to you."

There's no quick fix for sin, any more than there was cheap grace to enable forgiveness in the first place. But the choice is clear. We can rely on our own inadequate resources which, of course, compound our sin with pride! Or we can kneel in humble gratitude before our Saviour rejoicing in His grace as He works transformation in us.

Jesus summarised it perfectly - "I am the Way, the Truth and the Life."

Be still and know that I am God

psalm 73

... their mouths lay claim
to heaven ...

Surely God is good to Israel, to those who are pure in heart.
But as for me, my feet had almost slipped; I had nearly lost my
foothold. For I envied the arrogant when I saw the prosperity of
the wicked. They have no struggles; their bodies are healthy and
strong. They are free from common human burdens; they are
not plagued by human ills. Therefore pride is their necklace; they
clothe themselves with violence.

From their callous hearts comes iniquity; their evil imaginations
have no limits. They scoff, and speak with malice; with arrogance
they threaten oppression. Their mouths lay claim to heaven, and
their tongues take possession of the earth. Therefore their people
turn to them and drink up waters in abundance. They say,
"How would God know? Does the Most High know anything?"
This is what the wicked are like— always free of care, they
go on amassing wealth.

Surely in vain I have kept my heart pure and have washed my
hands in innocence. All day long I have been afflicted, and every
morning brings new punishments. If I had spoken out like that, I
would have betrayed your children. When I tried to understand all
this, it troubled me deeply till I entered the sanctuary of God; then
I understood their final destiny.

Surely you place them on slippery ground; you cast them down to
ruin. How suddenly are they destroyed, completely swept away
by terrors! They are like a dream when one awakes; when you
arise, Lord, you will despise them as fantasies. When my heart was
grieved and my spirit embittered, I was senseless and ignorant;
I was a brute beast before you. Yet I am always with you; you
hold me by my right hand. You guide me with your counsel, and
afterward you will take me into glory.

Whom have I in heaven but you? And earth has nothing I desire
besides you. My flesh and my heart may fail, but God is the
strength of my heart and my portion forever. Those who are far
from you will perish; you destroy all who are unfaithful to you. But
as for me, it is good to be near God. I have made the Sovereign
Lord my refuge; I will tell of all your deeds.

Psalm 73 could be entitled "Life ain't fair" with verse 3 being an example of where the psalm heads - "For I envied the arrogant when I saw the prosperity of the wicked"; and then verse 13 - "Surely in vain I have kept my heart pure". Walking the way of Christ can seem strangely empty sometimes when you look around at those who look after no 1, gossip galore, make a packet, trample all over people in their ambition ... and seem to prosper all the more for it.

This seems to be particularly prevalent in the world of fashion I have inhabited for many years and where so many place fashion itself on a pedestal that justifies any behaviour, with righteousness and justice seeming a million miles away. These types seem to prevail and it's difficult to see things changing.

But God doesn't just love fashion and the people in it, He longs to transform it into the place of true beauty it could be. The same, of course, is true for all places of work ... and those who work in them.

Do you long to see this? I do. There's a sting in the tail though. It's up to us to be His means of transformation.

Even so, it needs to be in His strength and timing, and as we pray and wait to see God act, we need to gird our loins and look to Jesus, taking verse 26 as our own, "My flesh and my heart may fail, but God is the strength of my heart and my portion forever."

If we take these wonderful and powerful Psalms to heart, we will see beyond the immediate to a great day soon when God's kingdom breaks out right in front of us, in our places of work. We need to stick on in there and trust God to act. Verse 1 - "Surely God is good to Israel (His church today) to those who are pure in heart." Amen to that.

I envied the
arrogant when I
saw the prosperity
of the wicked.

A.M. Father God, as often, I'm not feeling at my most robust, but I want to see Your purposes working out through me today.

Strengthen me, that I may be Your hands, feet, voice; that I might be a transforming presence wherever I go, whoever I speak to, whatever tasks I am called on to carry out.

But I can only do this in any real way by the power of the Holy Spirit within me. So come, Lord Jesus, come, pour out Your Spirit on me this day. Amen.

P.M. Come, fill me again with Your power, Lord Jesus. I feel surrounded by those with more determination and energy than I can muster. But they seem to trample over everyone around them. I am determined to do things differently, with care and compassion. Grant me a pure heart, and wash me clean that I might stand firm amongst the crowd, but not be of it. And may Yours be the glory.

God is the
strength of
my heart

EVE. Whom have I in heaven but you?
And earth has nothing I desire besides you.
My flesh and my heart may fail,
but God is the strength of my heart
 and my portion forever.
Those who are far from you will perish;
you destroy all who are unfaithful to you.
But as for me, it is good to be near God.
I have made the Sovereign Lord my refuge;
I will tell of all your deeds.
Amen.

I lift up my eyes to the hills ...

... where does my help come from?

I lift up my eyes to the hills
- where does my help come from?
My help comes from the Lord,
the Maker of heaven and earth.
He will not let your foot slip
- he who watches over you will not slumber;
indeed, he who watches over Israel
will neither slumber nor sleep.

The Lord watches over you
- the Lord is your shade at your right hand;
the sun will not harm you by day,
nor the moon by night.
The Lord will keep you from all harm
- he will watch over your life;
the Lord will watch over your coming and
going, both now and for evermore.

We all go through anxious times. Psalm 121 encourages us that God watches over us without ceasing, stopping our foot from slipping and harm coming to us. That's good, and I have seen plenty of evidence in my own experience that bears this out. But I've not, yet, found myself in a place of on-going anxiety and my heart goes out to those who do. No doubt, in some cases, we need to confidently (and persistently?) claim what is promised in this Psalm and elsewhere - for Jesus has won the victory and we need to seek to live in it. But godly people do find themselves in an ongoing struggle (David, the psalmist, was one) and I want to stand alongside you. No easy answers, but the final verse of this psalm has something to say - "The Lord will watch over your coming and going, both now and for evermore". We may not see release today or tomorrow but God's in this for the long haul, for eternity actually, and will be alongside you as you emerge from the tunnel of anxiety, however many comings and goings elapse between now and then. So you're not alone - ever - and my prayer is that this may be a tangible encouragement if you are in an anxious place.

A.M. As I prepare for work today, I'm thinking of those who have not got a job. Watch over them, Lord, as they search for employment; and ease their anxiety. Bring alongside them those who can help, with direction, money or simply encouragement.

Where I am that person, show me Lord, who You would have me seek out and give me persistence and determination to make a real difference for them.

As I go into my day, remind me that I am fortunate to have work and give me energy to give my best at all times as if working for You. Amen.

P.M. I'm reminded today, Lord, of people and places in the midst of war and strife. I lift up to You those suffering pain and living amongst destruction. Bring healing to the injured, peace to the bereaved, restraint to the perpetrators, wisdom to the politicians.

Your word says that You will keep us from all harm and watch over our lives. But this does not seem to be the case in so many places and in so many lives.

I pray that You might act; that you might intervene to prevent fighting; that You might come to the aid of those caught up in something quite outside of their control. Come quickly, Lord. Amen.

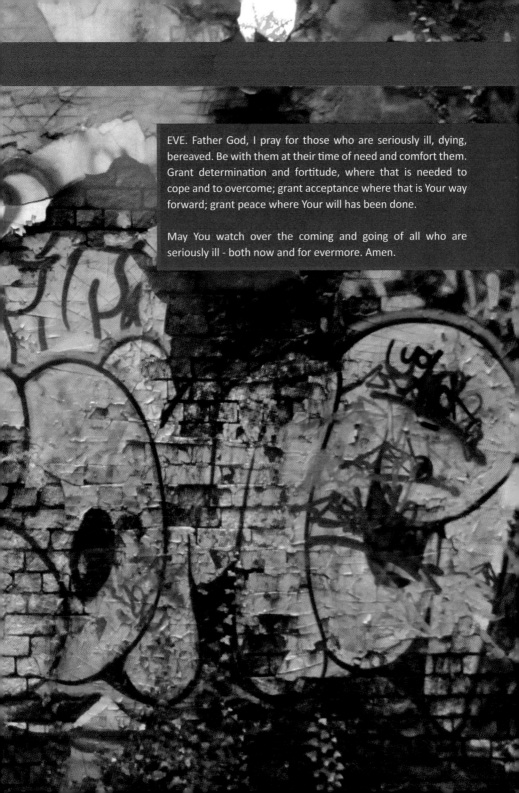

EVE. Father God, I pray for those who are seriously ill, dying, bereaved. Be with them at their time of need and comfort them. Grant determination and fortitude, where that is needed to cope and to overcome; grant acceptance where that is Your way forward; grant peace where Your will has been done.

May You watch over the coming and going of all who are seriously ill - both now and for evermore. Amen.

cycle 3

celebrate

psalm 67

May God be gracious to us

and bless us and make his face shine upon us

that Your ways may be known on earth,

Your salvation among all nations.

May the peoples praise You, O God;

may all the peoples praise You.

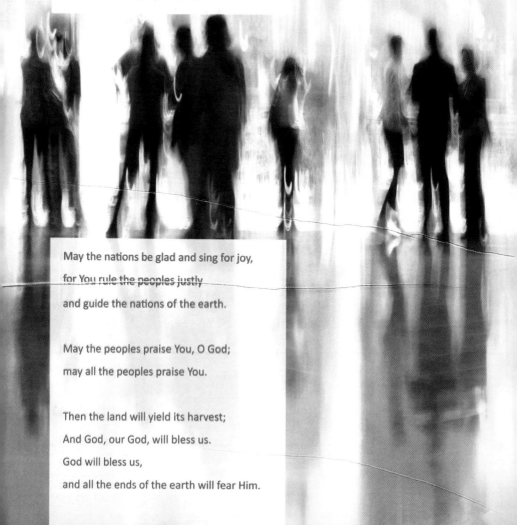

May the nations be glad and sing for joy,

for You rule the peoples justly

and guide the nations of the earth.

May the peoples praise You, O God;

may all the peoples praise You.

Then the land will yield its harvest;

And God, our God, will bless us.

God will bless us,

and all the ends of the earth will fear Him.

Psalm 67 starts and finishes with "May the Lord be gracious to us" ... "that the ends of the earth will fear Him". In between come "that your ways may be known on earth" ... "then the land will yield its harvest."

The story is very simple - God's blessed us to bless others. And an equally simple question is imbedded in this Psalm's overarching summary of the gospel - are we making God's ways known that the harvest will come? In its simplicity, the psalm is as stunning as it is challenging.

I write this during the inaugural London Collections Men, London's new Men's Fashion Week, which is a celebration of talented designers, but also a gathering of a great bunch of people (men and women) who are having such fun going about their work. This is in contrast to its high stress, big sister event, London Fashion Week, and shows that things don't have to be "same old, same old".

May the nations be glad and sing for joy

I can't help reflecting that, if an event can confound our expectation and be a matter for celebration, how much more exciting would it be if the praise of God could permeate this great industry called fashion. (Please substitute your own place of work here)

But it's not going to happen by magic. Those of us who have experienced the joy of knowing God's love and acceptance, need to be telling our stories so that others can join us in singing "May the peoples praise you, O God".

May we be those who are asking God to "bless us and make his face shine upon us", so that we might be unable to refrain from making Him and His ways known among our friends and colleagues.

Then the land will yield its harvest;
And God, our God, will bless us

A.M. Father God, I want to make the words of Psalm 67 my own. Be gracious to me and to all those who are dear to and close to me. Make Your face shine upon us.

May the reflection of Your glory in my face and behaviour be so bright that those I encounter will wonder what it is that causes this radiance.

Give me courage to give a clear account of the hope I have in Jesus that I might share Your blessing.

P.M. Lord Jesus, Your life made Your Father's ways known on the earth. Your death enabled salvation to be available to all nations. Saviour, I worship You.

As I have received Your blessing and favour, may I, in my turn, pass on this blessing. Then, and only then, will I play my part in seeing the land yield its harvest.

Give me courage, Lord, to make Your ways known to those I meet today; in Your Name and to Your glory.

EVE. Come Holy Spirit, and fill this land that Your ways may be known amongst all people; that Your just rule may give the guidance our nation so desperately needs.

Where there is hatred, bring love; where there is falsehood, truth; where weeping, joy; where darkness, light; where despair, hope.

May the fear borne of hatred that can flood our streets be replaced by fear of You, borne of love, true love that comes from You and You alone.

May the peoples praise You, O God, may all the peoples praise You. Amen and Hallelujah.

God, I worship

God of bustling city street. I worship

God of sparkling firework sky, I worship

God of grain of seashore sand, I worship

God of golden autumn leaf, I worship.

God of majestic cloud topped peak, I worship

God of distant moon and star, I worship

God of proud swaying field of corn, I worship

God of maker of tinned baked beans, I worship.

God of cocky urban rapper, I worship

God of legendary penner of plays, I worship

God of Sistine Chapel roof-painter, I worship

God of nursery school finger artist, I worship.

God of cuddly cat and dog, I worship

God of trumpeting elephant, I worship

God of spouting whale, I worship

God of ridiculous parrot, I worship.

God of the ages, God of the years, God of the
nano-second, I worship
God of the nations, God of our towns, God of
each van clogged street, I worship

Sing to the Lord a new song
Sing to the Lord, all the earth

God of glittering palace, God of comfy semi, God
of inner city slum, I worship
God of the famous, God of the hero, God of the
lost and bored, I worship.

God of abundant creation, I worship
God of patient, faithful grace, I worship
God of Calvary's flowing blood, I worship
God of eternal glory, I worship

God, I worship.

psalm 96

declare His glory

Sing to the Lord a new song;
sing to the Lord, all the earth.
Sing to the Lord, praise His name;
proclaim His salvation day after day.

Declare His glory among the nations,
His marvellous deeds among all peoples.
For great is the Lord and most worthy of praise;
He is to be feared above all gods.

For all the gods of the nations are idols,
but the Lord made the heavens.
Splendour and majesty are before Him;
strength and glory are in His sanctuary.

Ascribe to the Lord, all you families of nations,
ascribe to the Lord glory and strength.
Ascribe to the Lord the glory due His name;
bring an offering and come into His courts.

Worship the Lord in the splendour of His holiness;
tremble before Him, all the earth.
Say among the nations, "The Lord reigns."
The world is firmly established, it cannot be moved;
He will judge the peoples with equity.

Let the heavens rejoice, let the earth be glad;
let the sea resound, and all that is in it.
Let the fields be jubilant, and everything in them;
let all the trees of the forest sing for joy.

Let all creation rejoice before the Lord,
for He comes, He comes to judge the earth.
He will judge, He will judge He world in righteousness
and the peoples in His faithfulness.

"Declare His glory among the nations."
"Let all creation rejoice before the Lord."

The praise of peoples and nature intertwine through Psalm 96. To those familiar with the bible, this dual voice is familiar. But to the modern ear, the idea of fields being jubilant and forests singing for joy will sound like quaint picture language.

But I don't think the psalmist is playing with words here. Trees, fields and all creation are living entities and their very form and "living-ness" is an act of praise to their creator.

And, surely, things created by us creatures can similarly praise their ultimate Creator. Few would argue that the Hallelujah Chorus or a majestic cathedral stand as acts of praise to God. Of course it's not the skill of arranging notes or stones that make them sacrifices or praise, rather the intention of their creators.

What about in other spheres of creativity? Does a beautiful ball-gown "praise" God? Or a plain shirt?

I was very excited by a sermon - and thereafter reading Chris Wright's book "The God I Don't Understand" - which explored the assertion that heaven (up there) is not the final chapter. Rather, it is just a waiting room before the new creation is revealed (down here) on Earth. This new creation will be free of all pain, sin, frustration and failure and will feature, amongst other things, the best of all human creativity across the centuries ("the glory and honour of the nations" - check out Revelation 21 and ponder the imagery of what lies ahead). For those who watched the amazing opening ceremony for the 2012 Olympics, it was like a pocket sized warm up for the spectacular setting encompassing all human history that will be the backdrop for eternal life here on Earth.

Back to Psalm 96, all we create here and now which glorifies God will be woven into an everlasting tapestry. The reverse side of the coin of course, as other Psalms spell out with uncomfortable clarity, is that all the stuff which dishonours God will be burned up and thrown away.

So let's be done with getting ensnared by the gods of the nations which are idols (v5), and instead (v8) bring a daily offering that glorifies His name, whether creating that ball-gown, a white shirt ... or indeed an accurate set of accounts, or whatever it is that occupies us day to day. For these things will be the fabric of eternity as well as declaring, here and now, His glory among the nations.

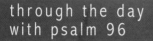

A.M. I want all I do today, Lord, to sing Your praise. May the quality of my work, the way I speak to people, how I approach challenges, rejoicing with others' successes, all point towards a God of grace. May my whole demeanour ascribe to You, Lord, the glory due Your name. And I will need to have my eyes opened to see what this looks like!

Take my life, and let it be consecrated, Lord, to Thee

P.M. Father God, this is a difficult one, especially if you like cars! Where does a car - and anything else come to that - stop being a thing of creative beauty and become an idol? It'll be the same for clothes, houses ... you name it.

I guess the answer lies in my attitude towards the item in question, and how easily I'd give it up.

Help me, Lord, to hold lightly to my material possessions and to focus my energies and desires on You, Your creation and Your Kingdom. That way, I will declare Your glory. Amen.

EVE. Let the heavens rejoice,
let the earth be glad;
let the sea resound,
and all that is in it.
Let the fields be jubilant,
and everything in them;
let all the trees of the forest
sing for joy.

Hallelujah, Lord, and I add my voice of celebration in worshipping their and my Creator.

psalm 136   declare His glory

Give thanks to the Lord, for He is good.   *His love endures forever.*
Give thanks to the God of gods.   *His love endures forever.*
Give thanks to the Lord of lords: *His love endures forever.*
To Him who alone does great wonders,   *His love endures forever.*

Who by His understanding made the heavens,   *His love endures forever.*
Who spread out the earth upon the waters   *His love endures forever.*
Who made the great lights   *His love endures forever.*
The sun to govern the day the moon and stars
to govern the night;   *His love endures forever.*

To him who struck down the firstborn of Egypt   *His love endures forever.*
and brought Israel out from among them   *His love endures forever.*
with a mighty hand and outstretched arm;   *His love endures forever.*
To Him who divided the Red Sea asunder   *His love endures forever.*
and brought Israel through the midst of it,   *His love endures forever.*
but swept Pharaoh and his army into the Red Sea;   *His love endures forever.*

To Him who led his people through the wilderness;   *His love endures forever.*
to Him who struck down great kings   *His love endures forever.*
and killed mighty kings -   *His love endures forever.*
Sihon king of the Amorites   *His love endures forever.*
and Og king of Bashan -   *His love endures forever.*
He gave their land as an inheritance   *His love endures forever.*
an inheritance to His servant Israel.   *His love endures forever.*

He remembered us in our low estate   *His love endures forever.*
And freed us from our enemies   *His love endures forever.*
He gives food to every creature.   *His love endures forever.*
Give thanks to the God of heaven   *His love endures forever.*

Psalm 136 tracks through creation, the exodus, and the time spent in the wilderness by the Israelites. It tops and tails with an outburst of thanks for God's person, provision and protection.

And you can't help noticing the refrain "His love endures forever" which comes after every line. The whole Psalm is one big praise-athon.

I have to confess that at first I found its repetitiveness boringly formulaic and more than a tad annoying. But then I remembered the old song "Count your blessings, Name them one by one, Count your blessings, See what God has done."

And I had to admit to myself that much of the time when I am out of sorts, it is because I have taken my eye off Him (and all that He has given to and done for me). Instead I have focused on myself and my "problems".

Back to the old song - "Are you ever burdened, with a load of care?
Does the cross seem heavy, you are called to bear?" Sound familiar?!

I think the Psalmist has got it right and we need to get into the habit of constantly recalling God's enduring love in everything we do. He does not grow weary of us, and if we respond with continuous praise, we will find ourselves in step with his steady faithfulness.

The song goes on "Count your many blessings, Ev'ry doubt will fly, and you will be singing, as the days go by."

I'll have some of that!
court.

Count Your Blessings

When upon life's billows you are tempest tossed,
When you are discouraged, thinking all is lost,
Count your many blessings, name them one by one,
And it will surprise you what the Lord hath done.

Count your blessings, name them one by one,
Count your blessings, see what God hath done!
Count your blessings, name them one by one,
And it will surprise you what the Lord hath done.

Give thanks to the
Lord of lords
To Him Who alone
does great wonders

Are you ever burdened with a load of care?
Does the cross seem heavy you are called to bear?
Count your many blessings, every doubt will fly,
And you will keep singing as the days go by.

When you look at others with their lands and gold,
Think that Christ has promised you His wealth untold;
Count your many blessings. Wealth can never buy
Your reward in heaven, nor your home on high.

So, amid the conflict whether great or small,
Do not be disheartened, God is over all;
Count your many blessings, angels will attend,
Help and comfort give you to your journey's end.

Words: Johnson Oatman, Jr.
Music: Edwin O. Excell

Thank you

Thank you for the morning skies that speak of hope and untapped opportunity
Thank you for the food and drink that sustain and strengthen for the day ahead
Thank you for the clothes that warm and protect and tell the world of who I am
Thank you for Your peerless Word, which feeds and guides and reassures
You love, You care, You provide unfailingly

Thank you for work to stretch and engage – wherever it is, paid or not
Thank you for colleagues to walk the journey – to share experience, sharpen skills
Thank you for new faces met on the way – whether fun encounters or times of testing
Thank you for old friends rediscovered – recalling those rose tinted good old days
You love, You care, You provide unfailingly

Thank you for the world that bustles around, the sights and sounds of busy streets
Thank you for the means of keeping in touch, through email, text and twitter and chat
Thank you for space, for peace and quiet, a still city church or parkland stroll
Thank you for rest at the end of each day, to pause and reflect on what's done or not
You love, You care, You provide unfailingly

Thank you for weekends and short breaks and holidays
Thank you for tv and music and movies
Thank you for museums, street cafes and pubs
Thank you for country walks, gardens and castles
You love, You care, You provide unfailingly

Thank you for friends and family, those closest around
Thank you for the Spirit, Who guides and empowers
Thank you for Jesus, who came, died and conquered
Thank you, Father God, for sharing Your precious world
You love, You care, You provide unfailingly

A.M. I start the day counting my blessings – an amazing morning sky gives You exuberant praise and shares it's joy with me and whoever chooses to watch. I may be in a city street or a windy hillside, but Your matchless Creation reaches everywhere. Thank you, Lord, thank you.

And thank you for cars that enable us to get around, for food, drink, central heating, gardens - the list is endless. Thank you, Lord, thank you.

For Your love endures forever, Amen.

P.M. Father God, You brought Your people through the wilderness all those years ago. But You are the same yesterday, today and tomorrow, so I can trust You to lead me through times of dryness and testing today.

I pray for Your people around the world who are struggling. Protect them in their trials and set them free from whatever burdens them.

Glorify Your name as Your redeemed people look to You. For Your love endures forever, Amen

His love endures forever

EVE. How wonderful is the night sky. It speaks of Your infiniteness, of Your majesty, that awesome time when You spoke and things started to appear – just how did that work?!

I praise You, Lord; You Who by Your understanding made the heavens; You Who spread out the earth upon the waters; You Who made the great lights, the sun to govern the day, the moon and stars to govern the night. It's simply amazing.

As I wind down for another day, I thank you for all that You have done for me, all that You have given me, all that You are to me. For You are everything to me.

Your love endures forever, Amen.

Pain at Remembrance

How can I believe in a God who let millions die in a trench?

Who looked on as millions more were condemned to the gas chamber?

Who didn't intervene as thousands drowned in sinking ships?

Who allowed my son to be taken out by a roadside bomb when he was in the prime of his life?

I'm so sorry that you lost your son; it must be desperately hard for you. This is such a difficult time for many people.

The Lord lifts up

You're right; there is much suffering in the world and I don't really understand why God seems just to look on.

I do know, though, that He gave us all free will to live our lives as we choose; other-wise history would just be a bizarre laboratory experiment.

And it is mankind doing the killing, not God. He is a God of love.

A God of love? Well, if he's that fussed, why doesn't he step in and do something about it?

If he's really there and claims to be all powerful, why doesn't he use that power to deal with all the wrongs of the world?

Anyway, what does someone we can't even see and exists out there somewhere, know about everyday life and suffering here on earth?

I do know your pain. I've suffered it too.

I lost my son. My only son.

Although it was many years ago, it seems like just yesterday. I still feel the pain.

But through his suffering, many others can be free.

And that makes his pain, and mine, worth it.

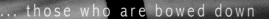

... those who are bowed down

psalm 146

As long as I live

Praise the Lord. Praise the Lord, my soul.

I will praise the Lord all my life;

I will sing praise to my God as long as I live.

Do not put your trust in princes,

in human beings, who cannot save.

When their spirit departs, they return to the ground;

on that very day their plans come to nothing.

Blessed are those whose help is the God of Jacob,

whose hope is in the Lord their God.

He is the Maker of heaven and earth, the sea, and

everything in them – He remains faithful forever.

Blessed are those whose help is the God of Jacob

He upholds the cause of the oppressed

and gives food to the hungry.

The Lord sets prisoners free,

the Lord gives sight to the blind,

the Lord lifts up those who are bowed down,

the Lord loves the righteous.

The Lord watches over the foreigner

and sustains the fatherless and the widow,

but he frustrates the ways of the wicked.

The Lord reigns forever, your God, O Zion,

for all generations. Praise the Lord.

Two questions.
Are you worn out?
What/who do you put your trust in?

Psalm 146 tells us that worldly ways and values will benefit us nothing, because human beings can't save. Even princes return to dust and all their plans will come to nothing.

Incessant striving is inevitably the way of a world that looks to itself. How else will anything get done? And this is an exhausting way of life. I know, I've spent too many years trying to do it all in my own strength.

But those whose hope is in the Lord, the Maker of heaven and earth, will see things differently. Their priority is not to strive to achieve, but first to praise their Lord in all they do, relying on Him to provide.

And if we are bold enough to choose this Way, praising God will remain our passion for as long as we live. For He remains faithful and, as we discover this, we will have no desire to return to relying on self and hard graft.

I hope that this doesn't seem just too simplistic or idealistic. Too many of us grind ourselves daily into the ground and we lose all freedom and joy ... and with it the energy and desire to point our friends and colleagues towards a wonderful God.

Take some time to rest quietly with the Father and feel the beat of His heart for you. It may shock but thrill you to know how much he longs for you to trust in Him and be set free from self-reliance.

Majestic Caernarfon Castle, built by Edward I in 1283 and the scene
for the investiture of the current Prince of Wales in 1969. Worth
noting though that, impressive though the walls are, it's an
empty shell and has been for centuries.

Do not put your trust in princes!

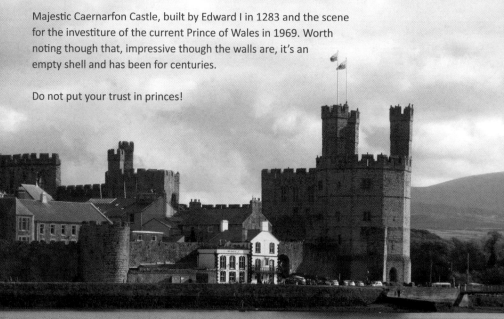

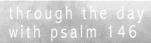

A.M. Father God, today I so want to live under Your guidance and in Your strength.

I read in Your Word how You walked with Your people of old and I put my trust in You, asking that You help me through today.

Blessed are those whose hope is the God of Jacob, whose hope is in the Lord their God. Amen.

P.M. Lord, how can it be that so many people, old and young, find themselves as refugees around the world?

Just as You watched over Your people in Old Testament days when they found themselves in foreign lands, watch over those who are displaced today. Strengthen the workers who seek to come alongside them in their plight.

Bring down those, princes or not, who would leave many in poverty to further their own ends. Amen.

EVE. I will praise You, Lord, as long as I live, for You are always there for me. You remain faithful forever.

Show me once again that I should put my trust in You, and Your leading, and not in the way the world would have me go.

For I know that is the way to freedom and fullness of life. And that is where I will find You. Amen.

He upholds the cause of the oppressed.

The Lord watches over the foreigner.

Footprints in the sand

One night I dreamed I was walking along the beach with the Lord.

Many scenes from my life flashed across the sky.

In each scene I noticed footprints in the sand.

Sometimes there were two sets of footprints,

other times there were one set of footprints.

This bothered me because I noticed

that during the low periods of my life,

when I was suffering from

anguish, sorrow or defeat,

I could see only one set of footprints.

So I said to the Lord,

"You promised me Lord,

that if I followed you,

you would walk with me always.

But I have noticed that during

the most trying periods of my life

there have only been one

set of footprints in the sand.

Why, when I needed you most,

you have not been there for me?"

The Lord replied,

"The times when you have

seen only one set of footprints,

is when I carried you."

Mary Stevenson

Praise the Lord. Praise God in his sanctuary;

Praise Him in His mighty heavens.

Praise Him for His acts of power;

Praise Him for his surpassing greatness.

Praise Him with the sounding of the trumpet,

Praise Him with the harp and lyre,

Praise Him with tambourine and dancing,

Praise Him with the strings and flute,

Praise Him with the clash of cymbals,

Praise Him with resounding cymbals.

Let everything that has breath praise the Lord.

2012. What an amazingly proud Olympics for us Brits. Not just in the astonishing success, but also in the humble way victory was handled. It's impossible not to draw a comparison with the call to run our Christian race with all we've got.

And this coincides with my arrival at the final Psalm in this collection, 150. It speaks principally in instrumental terms, but the message goes beyond music and is quite clear. There can be no half-heartedness in true worship or indeed true discipleship. Everyone, everywhere is to praise the Lord with everything they've got.

So, am I going all out for God ... or do I blow hot and cold? Pardon the directness, but are we actually, for all we like to think, "Sunday Christians" whose weekday lives are marginally distinguishable from those around us. Those who couldn't give a fig about their creator?

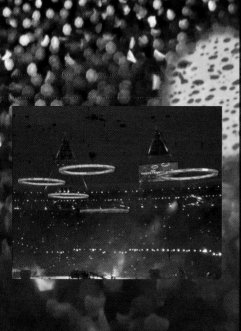

And I'm not pointing a finger at anyone here, but looking at the mirror and wondering what it would be like if I were to throw my natural caution and indeed reluctance, to the wind and speak and act like I'd love to ... but daren't?

Is a season coming where, if we want to see God's love sweeping across the world where we spend our days, it's up to us to speak out. To take on board and live out God's words to Joshua as he was preparing to enter the promised land? - "Be strong and very courageous. Do not be afraid; do not be discouraged, I am giving you the land and will be with you wherever you go."

The British Olympians (and of course all those great athletes from other countries) gave it their all; are we prepared to?

Praise Him in
His mighty heavens.

A.M. Lord as I look out at the morning sky, it proclaims Your glory. And I rejoice that I am known by You.

Lift my eyes throughout the day, I pray, so I can recall again and again Your majesty and faithfulness and sing Your unending praise in all I do.

Am I going all out for God?

P.M. Father God, I praise You for Your surpassing greatness. Everest is as big as it gets, but You are so much bigger! That's beyond my comprehension. And how do I reconcile that with Your tender, intimate love as You sent Jesus to Earth to deal with our sin on the cross? That's bigger still. Amazing.

Lord, I lay at Your disposal all my ambitions, abilities and resources. Please take them and transform them into something great that blesses others and glorifies Your name. Amen.

Praise Him for his surpassing greatness

Praise Him
for His acts
of power

EVE. When rivers burst their banks, they sure look mean. But all power is in Your hands and that is uncomfortable, even scary, as I like to be in control.

Sorry I always want to be at the centre. Help me to trust that I will achieve so much more with You in complete charge.

So, over to You. Lord, I will risk all and offer You everything.

Eternal yet here now, unseen yet ever present
Victorious yet broken, nailed to a cross yet freed from the tomb
Extraordinary yet everyday, complex yet simple
Righteous yet forgiving, holy yet accessible
Yahweh yet baby in a manger, Healer yet wounded
Trustworthy yet to be feared, constant yet ever changing
Humble yet mighty, loving yet just
Infinite yet intimate, powerful yet gentle
Name above all names yet became nothing
God within us yet over and above all things

This, and so much more, is our God
Let everything that has breath praise the Lord

Praise Him in His mighty heavens

Praise Him in His sanctuary

Let everything
that has breath
praise the Lord